Conspiracy Theories

Top 20 Conspiracy Theories

Norman Storm

NORMAN STORM

CONSPIRACY THEORIES

The follow eBook is reproduced below with the goal of providing information that is as accurate and reliable as possible. Regardless, purchasing this eBook can be seen as consent to the fact that both the publisher and the author of this book are in no way experts on the topics discussed within and that any recommendations or suggestions that are made herein are for entertainment purposes only. Professionals should be consulted as needed prior to undertaking any of the action endorsed herein.

This declaration is deemed fair and valid by both the American Bar Association and the Committee of Publishers Association and is legally binding throughout the United States.

Furthermore, the transmission, duplication or reproduction of any of the following work including specific information will be considered an illegal act irrespective of if it is done electronically or in print. This extends to creating a secondary or tertiary copy of the work or a recorded copy and is only allowed with express written consent from the Publisher. All additional right reserved.

The information in the following pages is broadly considered to be a truthful and accurate account of facts, and as such any inattention, use or misuse of the information in question by the reader will render any resulting actions solely under their purview. There are no scenarios in which the

Table of Contents

Introduction

Congratulations on downloading this book and thank you for doing so.

Conspiracy theories are an interesting topic, and many people love to learn about them, whether they seem far-fetched or not. Some will do research on the theories and find they believe them, and some are quick to denounce any theory as false, and sometimes outright ridiculous.

"Conspiracy" is defined as "a secret plan by a group of people to do something unlawful or harmful," and of course, a theory is just that: a theory. So a conspiracy theory is a hypothesis that there is a group of people secretly planning some harmful or criminal activity. The term used to mainly be used to describe any claim of political, civil, or criminal conspiracy, but has more recently come to be understood to mean a fringe theory that explains an event, either historical or current, as being carried out by a group of conspirators.

Some believe that conspiracy theorists are mentally ill, or otherwise unstable, whereas some see them as seekers of truth, as people who are able to see things, connections, that others may not be able to, and who are unafraid to speak out against the status quo. This book outlines 20 of the top conspiracy theories, going briefly into their history, the beliefs involved, and the reasons why. See for yourself: fact, or fiction?

There are plenty of books on this subject on the market, thanks again for choosing this one! Every effort was made to ensure it is full of as much useful information as possible. Please enjoy!

Area 51

What is Area 51?

Area 51 is a detachment of the Edwards Air Force Base. While the base itself is located in California, Area 51 is situated about 83 miles northwest of Las Vegas, in Nevada. The area is owned by the US Government and is operated by the US Air Force. The stated purpose of Area 51 is to develop and test experimental aircraft and weapons to be used by the US military. Area 51 is also referred to by other names, such as Dreamland, Paradise Ranch, Homey Airport, and Home Base. Military personnel often use the terms "the box" and "the container" to refer to the restricted airspace around Area 51.

Why is it so interesting?

The main reason that many people are interested in Area 51 is that there is a lot of secrecy surrounding the base. While there is often a lot of secrecy around any area that is testing and experimenting with new weaponry and aircraft for the military, some believe that the shroud around Area 51 hides deeper, even extraterrestrial secrets. One reason for this is that the US government will often not even acknowledge the existence of the base. They won't talk about it and don't address the area.

Another of the main reasons for the intrigue is the number of lights that people see in the sky above Area 51. People are told that the lights are due to the weapons and aircraft development going on in the base and that there is nothing extraterrestrial about it, but believers are not convinced.

It is believed that alien spaceships crash landed in the area, and were retrieved by military personnel. It's thought that much of the development and experimentation of weapons and aircraft done at the base are not on pieces of technology that had their origins here on Earth, but on the alien crafts that crashed on the site, including those materials they say were recovered at Roswell. It's said that scientists, employed by the military, are trying to reverse engineer alien technology for use by the military. Not only are they studying the crafts, but they're also examining the occupants that were found in the crafts, living as well as dead.

It's not only the study and engineering of technology that is said to happen at Area 51. Those who believe in the theory that strange things are happening there also believe that the government holds meetings with extraterrestrials there, and therefore secrecy and airspace restrictions are necessary to ensure that no one knows they are receiving visitors from beyond our planet.

Aliens aren't the only things that are said to be studied at Area 51. It is also believed that the government is using the space to develop technology that would make time travel a reality, as well as teleportation. They also believe that the government has been developing a way to control the weather and that they may already be using that technology today.

Many of the ideas of the strange happenings at Area 51 center around the underground facilities located at Papoose Lake or Groom Lake. People also believe that there is a transcontinental train system that starts at Area 51 and allows personnel to quickly, secretly, travel across the US. Also, the suspect is an airstrip that is said to disappear, dubbed the "Cheshire Airstrip," after the cat in Lewis Carroll's novels that disappears.

There have been several people that have said to have knowledge of things that support the conspiracy theories surrounding Area 51. A man named Bob Lazar said in 1989 that he was under contract to work with alien spacecraft that the government possessed. There was also a documentary in 1996 called Dreamland, directed by Bruce Burgess. It had an interview with a then 71-year-old man who was a mechanical engineer who said he used to work at Area 51 in the 1950s. The man said that he had been working on a "flying disc simulator," and that it was based on a piece of an extraterrestrial craft that was recovered from a crash site, and that was used to train US pilots. The man also said that he had worked with a being, not of our world, called "J-Rod," who he described as a "telepathic translator."

Another man named Dan Crain, who worked under the pseudonym of Dan Burisch, said in 2004 that he had been working on cloning viruses of alien origin at Area 51 and that he worked with J-Rod as well.

With all of the secrecy that surrounds Area 51, it has been easy for theories to crop up about what is really happening behind all those miles of fencing, all those guards, and even underground.

9/11 World Trade Center Attack

What happened?

On September 11, 2001, two planes crashed into the twin towers of the World Trade Center in New York City. Another plane crashed into the Pentagon, while yet another fell into a field. All told, 2,996 people lost their lives, and over 6,000 people were injured in the attacks. While it was a tragedy, many people believe it was not an accident.

What are the theories?

There are actually several different aspects of the theory that the attack on the World Trade Center was not a tragic accident, and that the truth has been covered up by the government. Below is a list of some of the theories that surround what is seen to be a mystery at the heart of the attack.

1. Stock Traders Knew About the Attacks Ahead of Time

It is said that right before the first plane crashed into the tower, many investors were expressing interest in selling American Airlines and United Airlines stocks. This is considered to be fishy because those were the airlines that were hijacked to carry out the attacks. It is believed by many conspiracy theorists that traders in insurance firms and the stock exchange were tipped off about the attacks ahead of time and used their knowledge to profit. Other than the obvious horror of using a tragedy to make money, this is considered suspect because they would have had to get their information from somewhere, and if someone knew that the attack was going to take place, why wasn't it stopped?

2. NORAD Issued Stand Down Orders

Another commonly believed conspiracy theory is that the North American Aerospace Defense Command (NORAD) had the ability to locate and intercept the planes, had knowledge of what was happening, and did nothing to stop it. It's said that NORAD scrambled fighters late so that the planes would be able to reach the tower and the Pentagon, rather than stepping in and taking the planes down before they could wreak havoc.

3. Collapse or Controlled Demolition?

One of the most common, widespread theories about the attacks on 9/11 is that the impact of the planes crashing into the World Trade Center would not have caused it to fall in the way that it did and that the collapse was, in fact, caused by strategically placed bombs within the building. This is called the "demolition theory." Proponents of this theory include architect Richard Gage, physicist Steven E. Jones, and engineer Jim Hoffman. These people say that the impacts and fires alone would not have been enough to bring down the towers and that they couldn't have totally collapsed, as quickly as they did, without other factors to weaken them.

An article was published in the Open Chemical Physics Journal called "Active Thermitic Material Discovered in Dust from the 9/11 World Trade Center Catastrophe," authored by Niels Harrit, Jeffrey Farrer, Steven E. Jones, and others. It said that there were thermite and nano-thermite composites found in the debris and dust around the collapsed buildings and that this is proof that they were brought down by explosives, not simply fires.

Proponents of this theory believe that the angle of the collapse and the heat inside that melted steel beams are proof that the buildings did not collapse due to the impact, but were instead demolished at the same moment as the impact.

4. No Plane Hit the Pentagon

This theory is backed by filmmaker Dylan Avery

and political activist Thierry Meyssan. They claim that American Airlines Flight 77 did not cause the damage and destruction at the Pentagon. They say that the plane didn't hit the Pentagon at all. Instead, they believe that it was a missile that hit the Pentagon and that the missile was launched from inside the US, with ties to the US government. Part of the proof they claim for their theory is that the holes in the Pentagon walls are too small to have been made by a plane as big as a Boeing 757. The hole was said to be only 60 ft across, but a Boeing 757 measures 155 ft long and 125 ft wide.

5. Fake Cell Phone Calls

Another claim made by those who say the attacks were faked is that the phone calls that were made from the hijacked airplanes during their doomed flights were faked. It's said that this is because cell phones could not get reception at the altitude that planes normally cruise. Another aspect of the calls that seems to prove them to be fake, or at least questionable, is that one of the callers, a son, referred to himself during the call to his mother by his first and last name, something that seems odd and suspicious.

There are many different theories that surround the possible faking of the terrorist attacks that took place on 9/11, and the ones listed here are only a sample.

The JFK Assassination

What happened?

On November 22, 1963, President John F. Kennedy was riding in an open-topped limo, traveling through Dealey Plaza in Dallas, Texas. He was shot, struck by one bullet in his head and another in his neck. A man was charged with his murder, Lee Harvey Oswald, and the Chief Justice, Earl Warren, stated that Oswald acted alone.

Why is it strange?

This is the story that is told in the history books, but conspiracy theorists believe a different, darker story. The theories surrounding the perceived cover up are about a conspiracy that involves the Mafia, the CIA, Vice President Lyndon B Johnson, Fidel Castro, and the KGB, either citing all or some of them as having a hand in the conspiracy. People also believe that Oswald did not act alone in shooting the president and that there was another gunman who fired the second shot.

There are as many parts of the perceived conspiracy plot to assassinate JFK as there are people who believe it, so only a few will be listed here for the sake of brevity.

One of the main components of these theories is that Oswald did not act alone, and the strangeness that was his own murder. He was arrested within hours of the shooting, and by the next day, he had been arraigned. By Sunday afternoon, Oswald was dead, having been shot by Jack Ruby, a nightclub owner, while he was being moved to the county jail from the city jail. Once he was murdered, people started wondering if the president's assassination was part of a bigger scheme.

Another component is the number of shots fired. The FBI concluded that three shots were fired, two hitting the president and one of those two hitting and injuring Governor Connally, who was in the limo with the president and others. Some believe that there was a fourth shot fired, from a nearby grassy knoll, that was actually the one responsible for Kennedy's death. This theory is backed by analysis of what is known as the Zapruder film, which is a silent 8mm film that runs for a total of 26.6 seconds. It shows what some believe to be the entirety of the assassination, but others believe that there is a break in the filming that could have shown more and proven that there was another gunman, another bullet fired. There were also eyewitnesses that said that there were more than three shots fired, including some reporters, one of whom said she was actually in the line of fire.

Another aspect of the shooting itself that comes under fire is the trajectory of the bullet in relation to the "single shot theory," which states that one shot fatally wounded Kennedy. Nurses and doctors at the hospital that the president was taken to reported that Kennedy's head seemed to have been hit from the front, as the back of it was blown out. However, critics have said that for the bullet to have followed the trajectory decided on by law enforcement, it would have had to change course after going through his neck in order to hit Connally where it did. Critics also say that the bullet traveled downward, which means that it was shot from above, from the sixth-floor window of the nearby Book Depository building.

Theories about the "why" of the conspiracy also abound. Some believe that the president was killed on the orders of his vice president, Lyndon B. Johnson, or by CIA agents, who were angry at the events surrounding the Bay of Pigs. Some believe that he was assassinated by operatives from the KGB, and others think it could have been mobsters who were angry with Kennedy's brother for helping to prosecute the organized crime rings.

Some people believe that Oswald was actually a CIA agent or that he had a sort of relationship with the Agency and carried out their wishes in assassinating Kennedy. An investigator for the House Select Committee on Assassinations said that those who were investigating had been put under pressure to not delve any deeper into the possible connection between Oswald and the CIA. He even said that there was a CIA agent in contact with Oswald in the days prior to the assassination, who had connections to a Cuban anti-Castro group.

The mystery surrounding the assassination of John F. Kennedy is one of the most enduring, widespread, widely believed conspiracy theories that exists in the United States today. There are many different ideas, reasons, and theories about it, and it warrants a closer look.

CIA and AIDs

You are probably familiar with the AIDs virus, but you may not be as familiar with the theory that it is not a naturally occurring virus, but is, in fact, man-made and was distributed by the CIA. It is widely believed and accepted that HIV and AIDS started in Africa, that it began as a monkey or chimpanzee virus which then "jumped species" to humans, and spread. However, there is a group of people who believe that the virus actually started out in Manhattan in 1979, which was a few years before the virus was noticed in 1982, in Africa.

It is believed by some that the virus began with the CIA, through inoculations against hepatitis B. These inoculations were developed with the use of blood donated by people in the US, the majority of whom were gay males. There was a study conducted that was supposed to be with the purpose of helping prevent hepatitis B in at-risk people, which the gay community was considered to be.

The study used blood from members of the gay community as well as a chimpanzee or monkey blood to create the vaccine, which was then administered to members of the gay community. Shortly after, when AIDs testing became available, doctors and scientists tested the blood of those who had participated in the study and found that many of them were infected with HIV. It's believed by some that the CIA intentionally engineered the virus, either to cull the gay population and bring back what they considered to be a moral majority or to simply use them as scapegoats to invent this disease for sinister use elsewhere.

Some also believe that the government invented HIV to thin the population, effectively committing genocide against its own people. An East German biologist published a pamphlet in 1986, during the first years of the AIDs epidemic, that said that there were scientists at a military lab in Fort Detrick, Maryland, who had created the disease by mixing a sheep virus called Visna with a retrovirus that causes leukemia, HTLV-1.

There are also those who believe that the AIDs virus was created specifically to cull the black population in America. They believe that there were scientists at a lab in New York called Cold Spring Harbor, who created HIV, and that the World Health Organization then used the smallpox eradication program to spread the virus secretly.

While there are many who believe that the virus was created intentionally for sinister use, there are some who posit that it was created by man, but accidentally. In 1999 a British journalist argued that a doctor at the Wistar Research Institute, named Hilary Koprowski, accidentally caused the epidemic because he used kidneys from chimps to make an oral polio vaccine. He claims that the chimps had been infected with the simian precursor to AIDS, SIV, and when there was a mass-vaccination experimental program done in the Belgian Congo, the virus jumped species.

Among the list of conspiracy theories is an idea that claims that AIDs is not a virus at all. Some believe that malnutrition is the cause of the disease in Africa and that promiscuity and drugs are what causes it in America. Some believe that AIDs is a Biblical plague, sent by God, in order to punish the gay community and the rest of America for allowing homosexuality in the country. These people believe that AIDs is specifically a "gay plague," and is their lot for their sins.

AIDs is a horrific disease that had left a scar on humanity and still affects people today, though not in the numbers that it wiped out whole communities of people during the epidemic. It's understandable that people would look for explanations for the horror, that they would try to attribute it to a single person or organization that can take the blame for such atrocities.

TWA Flight 800: Crash or Missile Attack?

What happened?

On the 17th of July, 1996, near sunset, Trans World Airlines Flight 800 took off from JFK Airport, heading to Paris, France. 230 people flew on the Boeing 747-131 jetliner that day. After only about 11 minutes into the fateful flight, the plane was flying at 13,700 feet above sea level, which is lower than planes usually fly at that point in flight. TWA 800 had delayed gaining altitude in order for another jetliner to descend. 11 minutes into the flight, TWA 800 was south of Long Island, New York, over the Atlantic ocean.

Right when TWA 800 gained clearance to climb and reach their cruising altitude, disaster struck. The plane seemed to explode, without warning. Kerosene was dumped from the tanks at the center and wings, and it vaporized in the air and then ignited. The ensuing fireball was seen all along Long Island, and so was sections of the plane falling into the water.

Why was it strange?

Right after the crash, there were eyewitnesses who were interviewed for TV and radio. They reported that they had seen something odd right before the plane exploded. They said that there had been something in the air flying toward the plane, a bright object, that had turned midair as it got close. They said that it moved horizontally as well as vertically. The fact that it was seen so clearly by so many people on the ground, from different directions, meant that the object had to have been near the plane, and not a case of optical illusion. It wasn't only eyewitnesses who claimed to see something strange in the sky, however. Other pilots flying at the time said that they had seen something near the plane, a bright light, right before it exploded. The plane seemed to have been shot down.

The FBI actually interviewed 154 witnesses that they considered to be credible, who all said that they had seen what looked like a missile flying through the sky toward the plane, right before it blew up. These people were school teachers, scientists, business executives, and Army personnel, and were considered to be able to be trusted in their opinions.

The government seemed to want to keep people from looking too closely at the debris. This also is said to point to a coverup. There was information leaked by the Navy and the FBI that seemed to imply that there was something dangerous on board TWA 800, something of a biological nature, that could be seriously risky for anyone to interact with. People reported seeing soldiers in bio-suits walking along the Long Island beaches near the crash site.

Officials claimed that there was no explosive residue found in the debris, but that was later said to be false information, and that the truth was being concealed by the public. Some people believed that it was simply a test missile gone wrong, but eventually, it was revealed that they had found explosive residue in the debris and that the missile had been live, not a dummy warhead at all.

The official story decided on by the government to explain the plane's crash was that the fuel vapors in the fuel tank at the center of the plane exploded suddenly, which blew off the nose of the plane. They say the plane then kept climbing, and that it was the plane's climb that people saw and mistook for a missile in the air. They say that the plane then exploded and fell into the water. Skeptics do not believe this story.

The official story doesn't line up with what many eyewitnesses, about 200 people, say they witnessed. It would require that every person who claimed to have seen something other than that story had been mistaken, that they had mistaken a plane climbing by itself in the air for a missile heading towards a plane.

21

Another reason why skeptics disbelieve the official story is that they say that a 747 without a nose could not stay in a stable flight long enough to make a climb the way the government said it did, and proponents of the theory say this has been proven to be false by calculations and model simulations.

People are also skeptical of the story because of the strange involvement of the Navy with the proceedings. As soon as the crash occurred, the Navy sent its best deep-sea salvage vessels to the crash site. They took over the salvage, kicking out the New York Police Department divers that were already there, and who had jurisdiction. Soldiers swept the beaches, while the Navy searched the bottom of the ocean in an area that is half the size of Rhode Island. The Navy explained its extensive involvement by saying that they couldn't find the flight recorders, also known as "black boxes," even though there were many private boat owners in the area saying that their sonar and fish finders were picking up the locator pings from the boxes. Eventually, the Navy admitted that there had been three subs in the area around the time that the plane crashed.

The government seemed determined to make the public believe that the plane just exploded out of nowhere, but many people are not convinced, and still believe that it was shot out of the sky.

Aliens and UFO Landings in America

There have been reports made all across the country of strange lights in the sky, strange vessels flying through the air, and strange crashes that no one seems to know anything about. These reports have been made for years, and have been brushed under the rug by the US government. However, there are many people who believe that the United States has made contact with extraterrestrial life and that there have been many landings and crashes on our soil.

Perhaps the most famous example is that of Roswell, New Mexico. Many theorists believe that what is referred to as the "Roswell Incident" is one of the most obvious pieces of evidence that the United States government has lied about and covered up contact with extraterrestrial life, here on Earth.

The event itself took place about 75 miles north of Roswell. Debris was recovered from a ranch after a ranch worker reported it. A press release the next day said that a "flying disk" had crashed on the ranch during a bad storm. Later, the story seemed to change. Now the press was saying that it was a weather balloon that had crashed, and reporters were shown debris that included foil, wood, and rubber, which seemed to confirm that.

According to official documents, the debris that was found on the ranch was from experimental technology, dubbed Project Mogul, which was supposed to detect sound waves present in the upper levels of the atmosphere from Soviet atomic bombs. However, many people do not believe this story. In the years that would follow, many books were published debunking it, claiming that it was actually an alien spacecraft that had crashed on the ranch, and that the weather balloon story was a coverup. Some claimed that there was a huge gouge taken out of the land at the crash site. Some said that witnesses saw an extensive, highly secretive recovery operation conducted at the ranch and that they were turned away by armed military police. One book claimed that there was a group of archeology students present who saw the alien wreckage, as well as bodies. People believe that it was an alien spacecraft that crashed on the ranch outside Roswell and that the government recovered alien bodies from the site, took them to a secured location, and conducted autopsies on them.

There have been other accounts of UFO landings in the US. One astronaut, Gordon Cooper, says that he witnessed a UFO landing at Edwards Air Force Base, in California. The story goes that he was part of a group of elite test pilots at the base, a group that was in charge of several advanced projects. He says that a camera crew was filming the installation of a system for precision landing when they saw a flying saucer in the sky. They watched it fly overhead, filming all the while and then saw it hover, extend three legs of landing gear, and come to rest on a dry lake bed. He said that the cameramen were able to get within 30 yards of the crash site while filming. He claimed that it was a "classic saucer," smooth and shiny silver. Further, he said it was about 30 feet in diameter. When they got closer to the UFO, he said it took off again. Of course, when the incident was reported to the government, Cooper was ordered to develop the film and then hand it over immediately to Washington, where it is now denied.

Those who believe that the government is covering up contact with extraterrestrial life believe that they're doing so because they have to keep covering the lies they started telling in World War II. Cooper says that they didn't want people to know about UFOs at the time, to keep the public from panicking, because they may have mistaken them for powerful enemy technology that the US couldn't defend against, which would hurt morale. Cooper says they continued to hide the existence of UFOs throughout the Cold War, and that they had to keep lying to cover up the old lies, and now they can't go back on them, even in the face of what many consider to be damning evidence.

There are many people in the United States today

that believe that we have been visited many times over by intelligent life from beyond our planet, throughout the years. Some believe that these visitors are actually angels, coming to protect mankind. Some believe that they are the origin of all life on Earth, that we humans actually descend from extraterrestrial life. Some think that aliens are basically gods, that they formed life on Earth and come back to watch over it. And some simply believe that they are intelligent life come to parlay with us, to bring us out into the universe.

Apollo Moon Landing: Faked?

On July 20th, 1969, the Apollo 11 was the very first manned mission to make it to the moon. Neil Armstrong and Buzz Aldrin were the first men ever to step foot on the moon. That is if they actually did go to the moon at all. There are many people who believe that the first moon landing, and the subsequent landings, were all faked. There are several reasons why people doubt the truth of the landings, and why the government would want to fake the landings in the first place.

Those who doubt that we landed on the moon say that the main reason the government would fake it is that they were getting desperate to beat the Russians in the space race, but we were nowhere near being able to launch a spacecraft that could support humans and make it to the moon in 1969. If we could land on the moon, we would be seen to have advanced technology, as well as the money required to fund such an undertaking. With the Cold War quietly raging on, the US wanted to prove that we were strong and secure enough to take the risk of sending people to the moon. Doubters say that because our technology wasn't where it needed to be, the government faked the moon landing.

Others claim that NASA faked the first and subsequent moon landings to make sure that it kept

28

receiving funding. Many theorists believe that it was not possible for us to get men to the moon in 1969, so they say that the money NASA raised for the project, around $30 billion, actually could have gone to paying off people that they owed. Doubters say that NASA also faked the landings to fulfill the goal set by President Kennedy, who said in 1961 that he planned to land a man on the moon and bring him safely back to Earth before the decade was out. Time was running out, and NASA had to do something to save face. Skeptics say that something was faking the landing.

Another reason people say there was a motive to fake the landing was that it was to distract the public from the very unpopular Vietnam War. People were so focused on the space race and so hopeful and excited about seeing someone walk on the surface of the moon, that the government was able to continue with the war efforts without as much of a backlash. Proponents of this theory say that it makes sense because the manned landing efforts seemed to suddenly end as soon as the US stopped being involved in the war.

There are many examples of what skeptics consider to be proof that the landings were faked. For the sake of brevity, there will only be a few listed here, but much more information about the theories can be found.

Many people look at the photographs and films that were taken while supposedly on the moon. Some point out perceived flaws in the images themselves, while some believe that the temperature on the moon would not have allowed for photographs or filming at all, that it was too hot and the film would have melted. Skeptics say that since there are no stars in the photographs, that means that the astronauts were not in space, especially since the astronauts themselves stated in a press conference after the mission that they hadn't seen any stars with the naked eye, either. Skeptics also say that the shadows are odd in the photos and film, that the color of the shadows, as well as their angles, are not consistent. Possibly the most famous piece of proof used by skeptics is the images of the American flag that was set on the moon during the first landing. Proponents of the theory that the landing was faked say that the flag appears to wave in the wind, which should be impossible, being that there is no atmosphere on the moon.

Other reasons people say the landings were fake include environmental factors. Skeptics say that astronauts could not have survived the trip to the moon because it would involve going beyond the Van Allen belts. The Van Allen belts trap radiation in magnetic fields, and proponents of this theory say that the radiation level going through and then past the belts would have posed health threats. They also say that this radiation level would have interfered with the camera film, causing it to fog up. Another point is that people say that the footprints that were left in the dust on the moon were not possible, as it requires moisture to make a footprint like that, that retains its shape. There is no water on the moon, and so, therefore, people say that the footprint was impossible.

There are many reasons why people believe that we have never landed on the moon, and many examples they can give as proof. It is an interesting topic, and one well worth researching further.

Reptilian Rulers

You may think you know who is in charge. You may be familiar with the president, the vice president, kings and queens in other countries. You may think they wield the ultimate power to shape our lives. Many people believe that you are wrong. There are those who hold the belief that there is a race of reptilian creatures that actually control the planet, and that these creatures have infiltrated our society to the point where we cannot recognize them.

There are two different origins stories that are widely believed. The first is that the reptilians evolved on Earth, alongside our other life forms. The theory then goes that they mastered intergalactic travel and left Earth, only to return millions of years later to control us and influence the course of our development. The other origin theory is that they originally came from a planet in the Draco constellations and that they came here thousands of years ago, sharing the planet with us. The eventually went undercover, either by choice or force and hid from us.

Proponents of this theory also say that they interbred with humans and that they have altered our DNA. They say that the reptilians did this so that we wouldn't be able to use our brains to their full capacity, which would make it easier for them to control us. The second reason they say they altered our DNA is to enable them to possess us, and that those who have been possessed by reptilians in the lower fourth dimension were considered demigods. They say that these hybrids gained power in such ancient civilizations as Mesopotamia, Sumer, and Babylon, and then they insinuated themselves into the royal families around the world as humanity grew up.

People who follow this theory say that the reptilians have power in every country around the world and that they've created a prison that stretches across the globe to contain and control humans, without humans even realizing what's being done to them. They say that they did this by creating borders, which gave humans something to fight over, and by controlling the media and distracting us with politics and entertainment. Proponents of this theory also claim that the reptilians are poisoning the water, food, and even air, in order to make humans more lazy and stupid, and therefore more easy to control.

According to this theory, and to many who believe it, there are two different types of reptilians at work in our society. Those who are pureblood and know they are reptilians, who can change their appearance to seem human. And, those who believe that they are human but are actually a crossbreed between reptilian and human, and are controlled to push an agenda that would bring forth the New World Order.

It is believed that you can tell which humans are actually reptilians by their appearance. They are said to usually appear as white people, with green, blue, or hazel eyes that seem piercing. They have scars that are unexplained, as well as lower blood pressure. It's said that reptilians don't have empathy, and are unable to express love the way humans do. They are also said to be very smart and to harbor a love for science and space. People say that you can try to see the reptilians' true form by watching TV in slow motion, to glimpse distortion in the image, scaliness or greenness of their skin, or reptilian eyes.

There are many people who are suspected to be reptilian. These include families like the Rockefellers and the Rothschilds, as well as the House of Windsor in Britain. People also think that many of the presidents have been reptilian, including Barack Obama, both Bush Sr. and Bush Jr., and Bill and Hillary Clinton. Proponents of this theory also believe that many entertainers are actually lizard people, such as Brad Pitt and Bob Hope.

Reptilians are said to consume blood, as well as brains. Theorists say that they actually prefer children, as they're not as full of poison as adults are.

People who believe this theory cite the Bible as proof. There are passages in the Bible that refer to humans interbreeding with Nephilim, and while the translation of that word is not certain, it can be said to mean "Those Who Have Descended." Since theorists believe that the reptilians are from another planet, or that they left and then came back, they are considered to have descended from the heavens. They believe that the Nephilim were not angels, as many Christians believe, but were actually reptilians, who bred with humans. The passage goes on to say that the offspring of these unions were considered heroes and men of renown, which is said to be proof that reptilians went on to be influential figures even into our time.

Holocaust Denial

From 1941 to 1945, Adolf Hitler ordered the systematic murder of about 6 million Jewish people. It is considered to be the deadliest genocide in history and was a part of a broader group of actions taken by the Nazi party of Germany to oppress and kill different political and ethnic groups throughout Europe. There are estimated to have been about 200,000 people responsible for carrying out the actions that robbed that many people of their lives. The Holocaust was a concerted effort by Adolf Hitler to eradicate the Jewish race, which he viewed as inferior. He actually viewed many groups inferior and sought to wipe them all out. I was horrific, and survivors of the death camps that remain alive today still remember the pain and suffering that happened there.

However, there is a surprising number of people who do not believe that the Holocaust occurred at all. These people have several reasons for this belief, and things they consider to be proof.

One of the reasons that Holocaust deniers say the myth exists is that the Jewish people created it for their own gain, to basically "cash in" on it and make money off of the restitution that would be paid by Germany afterward. They also say that the Allies perpetrated the myth in order to justify occupying

Germany in 1945. They say that there is a huge conspiracy between the Allied powers, the Jewish people, and Israel, to use the Holocaust for their own end, and to justify establishing the State of Israel.

Holocaust deniers are able to look past what many consider to be incontrovertible evidence that it happened, and say that it was all a hoax. They say that the Allied powers tortured those who took part to confess their roles and that the confessions were all lies that were spoken to save themselves from further torture. They say that the "few" Jewish people who actually died during this time died of natural causes, or were executed for crimes.

One of the reasons deniers say that the Holocaust didn't happen is that the gas chambers would not have worked the way they were built. They say that, as the chambers were not hermetically sealed, the gas would have leaked out and actually poisoned those trying to do the gassing. They also say that there is no way that the number of Jewish people who died is correct, as they say, that the mass graves and piles of bodies have not been found in the numbers that are reported by authorities and historians. They say that the Jewish people who were said to be starving in the camps were only starving because the Allies had cut off food supplies, and it was not perpetrated by the Germans at all. They say that the tattoos that survivors bear are faked, that the Germans would not have gone through the trouble of tattooing prisoners that they planned to slaughter. They say that the ovens that were present were too small to cremate bodies on a mass scale, and were instead there to cremate those who died of contagious diseases while working in POW camps during the war. They say the photos were falsified, as propaganda.

They explain the disappearance of that many Jewish people by saying that they actually immigrated to the United States, simply traveling out of Germany before things with the war got too bad and set up profitable shops and businesses in the US and other countries.

It seems unthinkable that the Holocaust did not occur, but there are many who believe that to this day and defend their viewpoints very vehemently.

The holocaust of the Jews was not the first or the last extermination to be questioned. A group of people that are responsible for atrocities may go through denial since it is unthinkable and undefendable what they did. Such is the case with the Turkish genocide of the Armenians in Turkey during World War I (1914-1918). There are numerous news reports in the New York Time and many other publications with pictures and stories of how the Turks slaughtered all the men and boys and walked the women and children out into the desert to die or to sold to local tribes. To this day the Turkish government will not admit their involvement in the slaughter of over 1 million Armenians even through numerous survivors have come forward and told their stories. People can do terrible things, and then they have to lie and lie to themselves about it. What is amazing is not only does the Turkish government deny any involvement, but they say it simply did not happen. It is also about the money too. If the Turkish government were to admit that they were involved, they might have to pay reparations and give back property that was owned by Armenians at the time of the genocide.

Did Shakespeare Exist?

To be or not to be? That is, apparently, the question when it comes to William Shakespeare. He is possibly the most well-known playwright of our age, but there are those who believe that he did not exist or, at the very least, that he did not author all of the works that are attributed to him.

Doubt about Shakespeare's identity first started popping up around the late 19th century, but since then the theory has basically gone mainstream. The former artistic director of the Globe Theater in London, which is a modern replica of Shakespeare's own theater that puts on plays, worked with a Shakespearian actor to publish a "Declaration of Reasonable Doubt," in which they say that there is room for doubt about the identity of Shakespeare. People involved in this work, or who signed off on its validity, include such people as the former LA *Times* art editor, an English professor at Washington State, and a social theory professor at Rutgers.

Theorists believe that there are many pieces of evidence that back them up, and what makes this discussion tricky is that William Shakespeare was so bad at leaving evidence of his life behind. He didn't sign almost any of his work, and the works he did sign show signatures so sloppy and illegible, they're hard to make out as his at all. They haven't found any letters or poems or plays that were actually written in Shakespeare's own hand, and his will makes no mention of plays or books, or anything else that would say that the man known as William Shakespeare, a balding businessman from Stratford, was a writer.

There is not much known about William Shakespeare biographically. The basic facts are that he was born, raised, and buried in Stratford-Upon-Avon, a market town around 100 miles northwest of London. Stratford was known for slaughtering and marketing sheep, and for wool trading and tanning. His father was a glover, and his mother was a member of the local gentry. They both signed their names with marks, rather than signatures, indicating a lack of education, and there's no evidence that either of Shakespeare's daughters was literate. Those who believe Shakespeare did not author his works say that his background wasn't compatible with the background of the type of person who would write the things he is said to have written. The person who wrote those works is said to have displayed knowledge of court culture and politics and sports beloved by the aristocracy, like lawn-bowling, falconry, and tennis. Believers of this theory say that the son of a glover was not likely to have experience with these things.

Most theorists, or Anti-Stratfordians, believe that William Shakespeare was a front or a pseudonym used to hide the real author or authors, who could not or would not, for whatever reason, take credit for their work. There are many people who Anti-Stratfordians say actually wrote Shakespeare's work, and here are a few of them.

Christopher Marlowe

Christopher Marlowe, also a playwright, was writing around the same time that Shakespeare was. Proponents of the theory say that Christopher Marlowe didn't actually die in a brawl at the end of May in 1593 and that this report was faked, in order to protect Marlowe from being imprisoned for atheism. People who believe in this theory, called Marlovits, think that Shakespeare was cited as the author of works Marlow actually wrote, in order to hide the truth that Marlow was still alive.

Edward de Vere

This important man, the Earl of Oxford and the Lord Great Chamberlain of England, was also a courtier poet. People believe that Edward de Vere could have been the actual author of Shakespeare's works because he had more of an intellectual background than Shakespeare did, with more experience in court and with poetry. Shakespeare's work seems to be written by a refined courtier with a good grasp on the intrigues that happen in a royal court, and people who believe Shakespeare did not write his works say that he didn't have the experience necessary to pen works with such a feel to them. They also believe that there are references in some of Shakespeare's plays that point to times in de Vere's life, and that there are codes in his works that say that de Vere was the actual author.

William Stanley

Another important person, and another Earl, William Stanley is seen as a contender for several reasons, one of which could seem very simple: his initials. Stanley was the sixth Earl of Derby, which would make him well-educated as well as familiar with the finery of court life. He also owned his own theater company, so he had a background in plays. Another point of interest is that he was known to call himself Will, as well as sign things with that name, something that William Shakespeare was known to do.

While almost everyone can agree that the works attributed to William Shakespeare stand the test of time as masterful works of art, some people do not agree that it was, in fact, William Shakespeare who penned them.

Chemtrails

If you've been outside on a clear, sunny day, you have likely seen the trails that are left behind in the sky by airplanes. These are generally understood to be "contrails," a portmanteau for "condensation trails," and have been explained jus to be condensation left behind in the air by the airplanes.

However, there are many people who do not believe this explanation at all. They believe that these trails are actually made up of chemicals, and call them chemtrails. They say that these chemicals are released into the air intentionally, for different uses, depending on the theorist. Some believe that these chemicals may be released with the purpose of controlling the population, manipulating people psychologically, modifying the weather, managing solar radiation, or chemical or biological warfare. People also believe that the chemtrails are the reason behind many health problems, including respiratory illnesses.

The theories began in 1996 after the United States Air Force released a report about weather modification. The report talked about weather modification, and afterward, the Air Force was accused of spraying mysterious substances over the population of the US. The accusers posted their theories on the internet, on forums, and the theories were also discussed by a late-night radio host. The EPA, the FAA, NASA, and NOAA all worked together to release a response to the rumors in 200, but believers of the theory just point to it as proof of a coverup.

So what are chemtrails?

People who believe in this theory think that chemtrails can be distinguished from harmless contrails by their appearance and duration. They say that chemtrails can last as long as half a day in the sky, or turn into clouds that are cirrus-like. Other markers of chemtrails are seeing a visible spectrum of color in the stream, a lot of trails in a concentrated area, or trails that linger after being left by military or unmarked planes flying at altitudes they wouldn't normally fly at.

Chemtrails are believed to have such substances in them as aluminum salts, barium, thorium, silicon carbide, lithium, polymer fibers, and other chemicals.

Those who believe in this theory say that people have reported seeing what they consider to be unusual activity in the skies. They say they've seen planes leaving trails behind at lower altitudes than normal, and trails that are parallel, ones that form S's and X's, as well as trails that spread out to make a hazy canopy overhead. They also say that they have experienced unusual tastes, smells, and even gotten sick due to the chemtrails.

What do the theorists believe?

People who believe in this theory generally think that chemtrails are part of a worldwide conspiracy. They say there are many different goals for this conspiracy, including population control, testing weapons (bioweapons, or using weather as a weapon), making people sick so the drug companies can profit. People also say that the government could be releasing vaccines into the air, to inoculate the population against their will, and say that this could account for some of the reports of illnesses due to the chemtrails since vaccines sometimes make people feel ill.

There are said to be thousands of reports, photos and videos that document the spraying of chemtrails, and the way that they stick around in the air for what seems to be much longer than contrails would. There are many, many people who believe this theory, and some parts of it may begin to seem a little eccentric.

For example, there are those who believe that chemtrails can be dispersed with the power of intention, that humans have the power to focus their will and intention on the sky and cause the trails to disperse. People also believe in beings called "sylphs," elemental beings that exist partially in the third dimension but mostly in the fourth. Who have the power to transmute air molecules into water molecules to isolate and fix the problems chemtrails cause, as well as round up all of these harmful chemicals they released into the air. These beings are said to be ethereal, not normally taking any visible shape, but that they can be viewed while they're fixing chemtrails. There are photos that are said to have captured the images of these sylphs all over the internet.

Paul McCartney is Dead

If you have kept up with pop culture at all during the last 50 or so years, you'll be familiar with a band called The Beatles. Considered to be one of the most influential music groups ever, The Beatles have enjoyed a fame unrivaled by many. With fame, comes attention, and attention often leads to more strange forms of attention, such as conspiracy theories, like the one that says the Paul McCartney is actually dead.

The rumor started in London, saying that Paul McCartney had died due to a car crash while driving his Aston Martin in January of 1967. Then, in September of 1969, an editor who worked on the student newspaper at Drake University published an article asking if Paul McCartney was actually dead. It detailed the rumor that had been going around campus that Paul had died, and those who perpetrated the rumor said they had found many clues in Beatles albums that had been recently released.

One well-known clue is that people apparently heard the phrase "turn me on, dead man" when they played a song titled "Revolution 9," on the *White Album*, backward. *Abbey Road* was released that October and the theory went that there could be clues found in the album art that pointed to Paul McCartney being dead.

The rumor grew quickly. A caller to a Detroit radio station told the DJ about the rumor and the clues, and a few days after that, *The Michigan Daily* published a satirical piece about the rumor, talking about clues that had been found on different Beatles album covers. He had made up some of the clues and was surprised when newspapers across the country picked up the story. The rumor just continued to grow, sparking a two-hour special on the radio, and inspiring a New York DJ to talk about it on the air for more than an hour, before he was cut off by being pulled off the air, for going off-format.

The story went that on November 9th, 1966, Paul McCartney argued with his bandmates during a recording session. He then drove off angrily, and crashed his car, dying as a result. To prevent widespread grief by those who were caught up in Beatlemania, the band replaced him with someone named William Campbell, a man who won a Paul McCartney look-alike contest.

There are said to be many clues that point to Paul McCartney actually being dead. Some say they have found hidden messages in Beatles songs when they're played backward, as well as forwards. For instance, people say they have heard John Lennon say "I buried Paul" at the end of the song "Strawberry Fields Forever."

Another clue that's often cited is the artwork on the *Abbey Road* album cover. People have interpreted it to be depicting a funeral procession, and say that Lennon, having been dressed in all white, symbolises a heavenly figure, George Harrison, wearing denim, symbolises a grave digger, Ringo Starr, wearing black, stands for the undertaker, and Paul McCartney himself, being barefoot and not in step with the rest of his band, stands for the corpse itself. People also say that a car's license plate that can be seen in the background is symbolic as well, for it reads "28IF." They said that means that McCartney would have been 28 years old at that point if he had lived.

This theory has been referenced in pop culture many times over the years since it gained popularity. A Batman comic in the 1970s referenced it in the plot. There have been several books released about the theory, and in 2010 there was a novel released by an American author that had all the Beatles as zombies, except for Ringo Star, and was about a zombie invasion in Britain. There was even a mockumentary released that same year, making fun of the theory, that had faked audiotapes of a person who claimed to be George Harrison, stating that the rumor was actually true.

Jesus and Mary Magdalene

Many people are familiar with the story of Jesus of Nazareth from the Christian Bible. He was born in Bethlehem, the son of Mary, who was a virgin and who immaculately conceived Jesus. He was raised by Mary and her husband Joseph, who was a carpenter. As Jesus was conceived in Mary by the Holy Spirit, he was not a human; Christians consider him to be one of the three parts of the Holy Trinity that make up God in three parts: God the Father, God the Son (born as Jesus), and God the Holy Spirit, who often appeared as flames or a dove. Jesus was raised just like any other boy at the time but soon started performing miracles. He was eventually crucified by the Romans, and rose again three days later, before finally ascending to Heaven. Jesus had many followers, called disciples, and close followers called apostles.

One such apostle that was spoken of in the Bible was a woman named Mary Magdalene. She wasn't talked about in great detail, which is part of the reason there are theories about her; there has been a lot left unanswered about her relationship with Jesus. One such theory is that Jesus and Mary Magdalene may have been married, and may have even had children together.

Mary Magdalene had at one point been possessed by seven demons, according to the Gospel of Luke, and they had gone out of her. It is said that her affliction wasn't actually demonic possession and that the demons may have stood for the severity of her sins or affliction. It's also said that Mary Magdalene was a prostitute. Either way, she was a woman with a low reputation when she met Jesus, and she came in where Jesus was dining with a Pharisee. She fell on her knees, weeping, and used her tears to clean Jesus' feet, then wiped them off with her own hair. Jesus saw the love in her actions and told her that her faith had saved her, and to go in peace.

Proponents of this theory say that it was written in the Gospel of Philip that this occurred, one of the Gnostic Gospels that were not included in the final version of the Bible. These gospels' authenticity has long been disputed by religious scholars and experts, but theorists say that there is merit in it. In the Gospel of Philip, Mary Magdalene is talked about as being closer to Jesus than any of his other apostles and is actually referred to using a Greek word for "companion," *koinonos*.

Peter also tells Mary in the scripture that Jesus loved her above all other women, which some have interpreted to show that the other apostles may have been jealous of Mary's closeness with Jesus, highlighting exactly how close she was with him. Jesus is also mentioned kissing Mary Magdalene fairly often. The fact that Mary washed Jesus' feet with her hair is also seen as a sign of intimacy because this was a time when a man only saw a woman's hair down like that in the privacy of their own home. Their intimacy is also seen by the fact that Mary Magdalene was the first person Jesus spoke to after he rose from the grave.

Proponents of this theory say that Jesus and Mary Magdalene had children and that their bloodline is one of the best-kept secrets of the Christian church to this day. They say the secret had to be kept because the Church would not have been able to control women as well if women had seen an example of such a strong female figure in the Biblical canon, as well as a woman who was considered to be Jesus' equal enough to marry and procreate with. Some have said that the Gospel of Philip doesn't show Mary Magdalene as being a prostitute at all, but rather a woman of stature who was seen almost as a goddess in the years to come. She would have been given too much power through this Gospel for the church to allow it to become part of the Bible. They also believe the Church would not allow this knowledge to become mainstream because it would paint Jesus in a more "human" light, as someone with base urges who gave into his fleshly desires, rather than the pure and holy Son of God.

This theory was famously part of the book *The DaVinci Code* and has been discussed in many books, movies, and other publications.

Illuminati

If you're familiar with any conspiracy theories at all, you have likely heard the term "Illuminati" before. Many conspiracy theories go back to the Illuminati. Indeed, many of the ones discussed in this book are also said to be related to the Illuminati. But what exactly is it? Historically, the Illuminati actually existed. It was called the Order of the Illuminati and was a secret society in the Enlightenment age in Upper Bavaria, in Germany. It was founded by a university professor named Adam Weishaupt in 1776 and was a group of people who advocated such things as secularism, freethought, liberalism, gender equality, and republicanism. They recruited their members from the German Masonic Lodges, which were mystery schools to teach rationalism. The Order was not long-lived, however, and was broken up and suppressed by government agents. The government was afraid of groups of this kind, as they were breeding grounds for the types of people who would try to overthrow what they perceived to be an unjust government.

However, according to some, the Illuminati never died, but simply went further underground, and still exists to this day. There are many, many facets of this theory, and proponents say that the Illuminati's influence reaches everywhere, into many different aspects of our lives.

CONSPIRACY THEORIES

According to some, the Illuminati is a group of elites who work from the shadows to control almost everything having to do with our lives, everything from the government and finances to culture and religion. People believe that, although membership is secretive and no one can be sure who is in the Illuminati, many members leave signs for those in the know to find. People who are suspected of being in the Illuminati range from Barack Obama, the Pope, Queen Elizabeth II, and George W Bush, to Kanye West, Lady Gaga, Jim Carrey and Willow Smith. The banks are all supposedly in on it, with their highest-ranking leaders in the Illuminati.

The Illuminati is said to control many different things, or at the very least, influences things. They are said to order assassinations, and it's believed that they ordered John F Kennedy's assassination, because they were afraid of him making too many changes to the Federal Reserve. The Illuminati is also said to control the Federal Reserve, in order to control all finances in the United States, and even beyond. It's said they manipulate the currency, in order to keep the rich right where they are and keep the poor from gaining wealth.

People also believe that the Illuminati controls the media, and uses it to further their agenda, by making the public believe whatever they want us to believe. They also use the media to keep us complacent and distracted, so we won't notice what they're up to, and how they're controlling our lives.

Those who believe in this theory believe that the Illuminati's end goal is to establish a new worldwide authoritarian government, called the New World Order. There are as many theories about what will come next as there are theories about the Illuminati itself. Some believe that the Illuminati is Satanic, and the members wish to bring about the reign of Lucifer on the Earth. They believe that an Antichrist will emerge to plunge the world into darkness, to control everything for their gain. Most of the people who believe this are part of the more fundamentalist Christian groups, and they believe that this will bring about the End Times. Because the Devil is immoral, they believe that many of the goals of the Illuminati are to try to make everyone else be as immoral as the believers think the members are. For example, one theory says that part of the New World Order will be forced conversion to homosexuality. Many believe that the end goal is for the world to be controlled by a small group of "enlightened' people.

People believe that there are clues you can find to point to the existence of the Illuminati. Possibly the most famous of these is the All-Seeing Eye, which is a pyramid with an eye. It is featured on the reverse of the seal of the United States and is considered to be linked to the Illuminati, who believers say see all and know more than the rest of us because of it. The Eye is also present on the back of the $1 bill, which is said to be a sign that the Illuminati controls our currency.

There are also said to be clues left by many powerful and influential members of the society, who we know as celebrities. People like Jay-Z and Beyonce are said to feature the All-Seeing Eye and other Illuminati references, like words and phrases that point to a secret society or a new world order, in their songs and music videos. Actors also make up part of this group, and such people as Emma Watson and Bradley Cooper are said to be members.

NORMAN STORM

Fluoride in the Water for Mind Control

You may be familiar with fluoridation. It is the process by which the government adds fluoride to the municipal drinking water supply, ostensibly to strengthen bones and teeth, especially in children. It seems like a good program, for the benefit of the citizens. However, there are many who believe that the reasons for the introduction of fluoride into our water are much more sinister.

To start, they say, you have to understand the difference between the type of fluoride that human bodies need and can process, and the poisonous type they say is added to our water. Organic calcium-fluoro-phosphate is the good kind, the kind that we need to build and strengthen our bones and teeth, and it can be found in foods. It's an organic, edible salt, insoluble in water, and it can be assimilated into our bodies. This is not the kind of fluoride that proponents of this their say that the government feeds to us through our water. That kind is apparently sodium fluoride, a deadly poison. It is water soluble and not organic and can be used as a very efficient rat-killer.

The sodium fluoride in the water is said to have a number of harmful effects, from destroying teeth to effectively providing minor lobotomies to massive amounts of people. This is the main reason, people say, that the government distributes it in the drinking water. They say that the real reason for the fluoridation of drinking water is to keep the population more docile and less resistance to being controlled, to having their freedoms taken away. They say that, over time, the amount of fluoride in the water slowly poisons and kills a part of the brain, which makes the person drinking it more submissive to those in power.

There are many different theories about the origins of the fluoridation of our water supply. Some believe that it was a plan concocted by Hitler and his scientists during World War II, that was later adopted by the United States. Some think big business and banks are behind it, using the sodium fluoride to make their customers easier to control.

There are also people who believe that the type of fluoride put in our water is the safe kind, but that it's morally wrong. They say that it's like the government vaccinating its people against their will, without their permission.

Curse of Malaysia Airlines

You probably remember when Malaysia Airlines flight MH370 basically disappeared on March 8, 2014. It was en route to Beijing Capital International Airport in China, having taken off from Kuala Lumpur International Airport in Malaysia. The Boeing 777 made voice contact with air traffic control at 1:19 local time, over the South China Sea. This was less than an hour after takeoff. Two minutes later, the plane disappeared from the air traffic controllers' radars. Malaysia's military radar kept tracking the plane, watching it go off of its planned flight path, westwards and crossed over the Malay Peninsula. Soon after, it left the range of the military's radar. No one was able to find it, and no one heard from it. It was assumed that the plane went down, so a search effort began that spanned across seas and was a multinational effort. They still have not found the bulk of the aircraft, and no one knows exactly what happened to it, or why it went down.

There are many theories as to why MH370 went down, and who did it. Some believe that it was hijacked, either by outsiders or by the crew itself. Some say North Korea hijacked the plane Some people, like political commentator Rush Limbaugh, believe that the plane was shot down by a government entity. Some say it was a paranormal incident, with the passengers and crew having been abducted by aliens or time travelers.

Malaysian Airlines' troubles aren't limited to this one incident, however. They seem to have had more than their share of aircraft issues, and some believe that it is not a coincidence or technical issue, but a curse. Proponents of this theory cite the fact that the number 7 was related to every single Malaysian Airlines crash or disappearance as proof that there's something strange and sinister going on. MH370 was a Boeing 777, and it was carrying 227 passengers. On July 17, 2014, one of Malaysia Airlines' planes was shot down; it was also a Boeing 777, and the flight code was MH17. That plane had been flying for 17 years before it crashed. Going back further, they say, there was also a crash on December 4th, 1977, which was actually the first recorded aircraft crash. It was heading for Kuala Lumpur, and there were 7 crew members on board.

Then there are some who don't point to the number 7 at all, but still, say there is a curse on the airline. They say it began with the 1977 crash, which to this day has not been fully explained. Then, in December of 1983, Malaysian Airline System Flight 684 crashed on its way back from Singapore, just shy of the runway. In September of 1995, another Malaysia Airlines flight crashed, Flight 2133. Then in March of 2000, yet another Malaysian Airlines disaster occurred, when Flight 85 had a toxic leak.

NSA Surveillance

The idea that our government spies on us is one familiar to most people, and believed by many. The National Security Agency is a government organization that is dedicated to preserving the safety of our country, usually by monitoring within the country. For a long time, people have been uneasy about the idea that there is a government entity watching them, viewing it as an invasion of privacy. It was seen as a conspiracy theory, the belief that the government was secretly collecting information about its people, everything from physical images to bank records to cell phone calls. This is one of those theories that has been proven correct. Whistleblowers like Edward Snowden have come forward saying that the NSA has been using its surveillance powers to turn inward, to spy on United States citizens, by saying that they're searching for domestic terrorists or signs of foreign terrorists on our soil.

The apparently true conspiracy is said to involve such people as George W Bush, Barack Obama, their aides, members of Congress, executives and technicians at different computer server and telecom companies, federal judges, and thousands of NSA employees and vendors. This spying has been kept secret because the conspirators knew that it would be viewed as a crime, that such spying is a violation of the right to privacy. Some believe that the ends justify the means, and are okay with being watched it means the government can find threats more easily. Some, however, point to the secrecy as a sign that the government knows that what it's doing is illegal and morally wrong and that it's being done to predict our behavior and control us.

There are many different ways that people believe the NSA is watching them, some more likely than others. The government has admitted to tapping phones, so people believing that their conversations are being listened to and their text messages are being read isn't far fetched. There are also, however, people who believe that any trace they leave of themselves on the Internet, such as shopping history or opinions, is kept in a file in a government building. It's said that information is provided to the NSA from such large web presences as Google, Facebook, Yahoo!, Youtube, and Skype, and some people feel that the government is tracking their every move by looking at their internet history and usage of programs from these businesses.

PRISM is a program that used to be kept secret but has now come to light. The acronym stands for Planning Tool for Resource Integration, Synchronization, and Management, and PRISM has been used to collect and analyze a great deal of private data that's stored on servers operated by the companies listed above. The national intelligence director, James Clapper, said in 2013 that PRISM is a government computer system that they use to "facilitate the government's statutorily authorized collection of foreign intelligence information from electronic communication service providers." In a nutshell, it's a program that the government uses to obtain information from private servers, information that many people believe should be private. They say that PRISM and programs like it are unconstitutional and that there are many such programs that are kept secret by the government, so the people won't know just how much information the government is collecting on them.

Some people believe they are being watched, not only through their phone conversations and internet activity but through other methods too. Such methods include the government watching us through our webcams, tracking us using the GPS in our phones, listening to us through gaming systems that have voice recognition, like the Xbox One, and recording and storing images of us captured by security cameras all over the country. Some even believe seemingly innocuous games, such as Pokemon GO!, are tracking us and are being used to collect data on us.

This is an interesting instance of a conspiracy theory that many have believed for many years, that actually turned out to be, at least in part, true. There does seem to be a hidden conspiracy between government bodies and companies to collect information about United States citizens. Some believe that this is illegal and that the conspiracy continues in the fact that these groups are still allowed to continue with their actions, after having admitted them, without prosecution or risk of being shut down.

NORMAN STORM

Hitler Escaped Germany

There are many conspiracy theories that center around Nazi Germany. From U-boats full of treasure sunk off the coast of New Zealand to jungle hideouts to sunken gold in Austrian lakes, there is no shortage of unconventional beliefs about what happened during and around the time of World War II. One such theory is that Adolf Hitler and his wife, Eva Braun, did not kill themselves together in their bunker, but instead escaped Germany and lived out their days in South America.

This theory began because, while most scholars and historians agree that the suicide occurred, their bodies were never publicly seen, or formally identified. South America comes into play because, as Berlin fell, Latin America was welcoming Nazis fleeing from Germany, so it would have been the most logical place for Hitler to flee to.

This rumor was not only believed by fringe groups. It was actually spread by top ranking officials in both the Allied forces and the Nazi forces, and it spread like a virus very quickly in all of the confusion that came after the end of the war. German diplomats were promising that Hitler had fled and that he would return. In fact, the rumor was so prevalent that the FBI actually began looking into it actively. In 2014, the FBI released over 700 declassified pages of investigations and tips on the rumor that Hitler survived and escaped.

There were hundreds of notes to the FBI in the files, as well as memos within the government as they tried to verify the tips and claims, and J. Edgar Hoover's responses. There was one document that recorded the statement of someone who said they had witnessed Hitler's landing in Argentina, saying that he was one of four people who met the party as they emerged from submarines about two weeks after Berlin fell.

The files were full of such documents recorded supposed eyewitness encounters with Hitler. One person said that Hitler was actually living in Manhattan, hiding in plain view. Another said they had shared a table at a restaurant in Maryland in 1946. Still, another said Hitler was being seen by a doctor in Spain for what they called a "nervous condition." There was even a letter, translated into English from German, postmarked with German postage stamps, that was supposed to be from Hitler himself. The letter said that when he had heard that he and his wife's bodies had been burned, he couldn't help but smile because they were already on their way to Argentina at the time. The FBI considered the person who turned in that letter to be not credible, but according to the files, viewed many other letters as possible truth.

The FBI file ended in 1947, but the belief in this theory has not. Over 70 years has passed since the end of World War II, and there are still dozens of journalists, historians, documentarians, and hobbyists who believe that Hitler either escaped Germany and died in South America or is even still alive. There have been many books written on the subject, as well as documentaries made. One book, called *His Life and Death*, by Simoni Renee Guerreiro Dias, argues that Hitler lived out his last years in a town in Brazil, under the pseudonym Adolf Leipzig. The author says Hitler chose the surname after the hometown of his favorite composer, Johann Sebastian Bach. In 2010, there was a book published called *Grey Wolf: The Escape of Adolf Hitler,* written by Simon Dunstan and Gerrard Williams.This book claimed that Hitler escaped to Patagonia, where he and Eva Braun raised two children. It was eventually made into a movie.

Part of the reason for the widespread belief in this theory is the mystery around the bones found around the bunker after the war. Russia took bones from the Eagle's Nest, including a skull and a jawbone. They said both belonged to Hitler, but it was later revealed that the skull actually belonged to a woman. Russia still claims that the jawbone is Hitlers, that it matched his dental records. However, there are many who do not believe this claim and think that Hitler escaped, to live out the rest of his days in peace with his wife.

NORMAN STORM

Barack Obama is a Muslim Immigrant

Few will be able to forget the historic election of the United States of America's first African-American president in 2008. Few can also think about the election without thinking of the suspicions that were levied against Obama with regards to his citizenship and his religion. Many believed, and still believe, that Barack Obama is not actually an American citizen, which would disqualify him from being president, and that he is a practicing Muslim, something that many members of the right wing are bothered by.

The rumors began during Obama's campaign for the Senate in 2004 and spread through viral emails by 2006. Though he was raised by his Christian mother, for the most part, his father and stepfather were both Muslim, and this is one basis for the rumor. It was also said that during the ceremony for him to take his oath of office for the US Senate, he placed his hand on a Qur'an rather than on the traditional Bible. There were also rumors that he had spent four years in a Muslim seminary, or a madrassa, in Indonesia. This story was published in a magazine that has since stopped publication. There was another rumor that his middle name was Mohammed, and this was used to further the claim that he is actually Muslim. His real middle name is Hussein, but that has not really helped the case against him, as believers in this theory point to the very Muslim-sounding middle name as proof still, especially since Americans have been used to hearing that name in the context of Saddam Hussein.

The belief that Obama is a Muslim seems to be troubling to those to believe it because they feel that Islam is a dangerous, violent religion, deeply involved in terrorism and attacks throughout the world because of the teachings of the Qur'an. So, if Obama is a Muslim, that makes him a threat to the American way of life, according to believers of this theory. Some think that Obama was placed in office to wreak havoc from the inside out, to bring down the United States on behalf of what they consider to be the violent Muslim majority.

The other part of the rumor about Barack Obama's origins is that he is not a natural-born American citizen. Though he was born in Hawaii, many people believe that is a lie, used to cover up the fact that he was actually born in Kenya. Others believe that, since Obama lived in Indonesia for a time as a child, he became a citizen of Indonesia and lost his US citizenship.

These theories about Obama's religion came onto the scene around 2004 when Obama was running for the US Senate. The rumors spread on the internet and were also voiced in a press release by another candidate, Andy Martin, and they eventually evolved into conspiracy theories about his citizenship. Starting in 2008, there were rumors spread on conservative websites that said that Obama was born in Kenya and then flown to Hawaii. This would disqualify him as president, as one has to be born in the US to qualify for the presidency. Emails circulated that spread the rumor and went viral. Soon after, people began demanding to see Obama's birth certificate, and that's where these theorists got their name: birthers. A former Democratic State Committee of Pennsylvania member Philip J Berg tried to sue Obama and was unsuccessful. He claimed that Obama was born in Mombasa, Kenya. There were articles published that referred to him as "Kenyan-born," and anonymous emails claimed that the Associated Press had called him "Kenyan-born" as well.

In June of 2008, Obama's campaign released an image of his birth certificate, but it was rejected by conspiracy theorists, who said it had been digitally created using Adobe Photoshop. Eventually, a long-form birth certificate was released to try to quell the rumors, but it was again rejected by conspiracy theorists, who said again that it was a forgery. Even if it was an actual Hawaii birth certificate, some birthers claimed that didn't matter, because anyone could get a birth certificate from Hawaii to say they had been born there.

They also claimed that the birth certificates could not be valid, as they were printed on a laser printer, which didn't exist when Obama was born in 1961. There is a myriad of other claims birthers have made about the birth certificate that they say prove there is a cover-up. Such as, his mother didn't live at the address that was on the birth certificate. That it lacks the state seal, lacks an official's signature, lacks a certification number, that he was not born in a hospital, that his registration was created by his grandparents and not a physician, and even that he has a Canadian birth certificate, among many others.

On December 16th, 2016, Sheriff Joe Arpaio of Maricopa County in Arizona held a press conference regarding Obama's birth certificate. The Investigation concluded that Obama's birth certificate, which was released by the white house, was clearly a forgery. This was no wild claim. Experts were hired, and evidence of a forgery was presented. The investigation was started in 2011 and was concluded in 2016. Mike Zullo, a posse member, headed up the investigation and hired experts showed 9 points of forgery on the document. They also showed how Obama's birth certificate had elements which were copied from an existing birth certificate of another person from Hawaii. You can see the press conference on YouTube by using the following link: https://www.youtube.com/watch?v=jk3KRxTfkLM

It is interesting to note that Federal prosecutors and the Obama administration justice department was investigating Sheriff Joe Arpaio for many years in regard to racial profiling. Later they brought charges of contempt of court. Did Obama hear that Sheriff Joe was investigating his birth certificate and decide to try and "take out" Sheriff Joe? Just months before Sheriff Joe's press conference, The Department of Justice attorney John Keller accused Sheriff Joe of violating a preliminary injunction, dating back to December 2011, to prevent the Maricopa County Sheriff's office from following and enforcing federal immigration laws. The case was later turned over to the Justice department, which is fully under Obama's control. The DOJ charged the Sheriff with contempt of court. This was all happening during the reelection bid which Sheriff Joe lost.

Many have since dismissed the claims made by birthers that Obama isn't a citizen as simple racial prejudice, but there are still many people who believe that he was not born in the United States, and should never have been president.

One-World Government

This conspiracy theory actually brings together a group of others, including theories about the Illuminati, lizard people, and aliens. It says that there is a group of people, elites, who rule the world, and whose goal it is for the world to be ruled by a single government that they control, without having to hide in the shadows the way that they do now.

Those who believe this conspiracy theory believe that there is a group of evil people who want to rule and that they do so by subtly infiltrating our societies, tricking the population into believing them. They say that these people use distractions such as entertainment media, study, unnecessary work, and sports to distract us, so we won't realize that they're taking over. It's believed that this group of people is made up of international bankers as well as the Illuminati and that these people control everything: the workforce, mainstream media, education system, banks, commerce, energy, and even the governments. This group is said to be controlled by the super-rich, families like the Rothschilds and the Rockefellers. They're also said to hide behind organizations like the United Nations, which many people believe is actually a form of one-world government.

Believers feel that this group has several goals. Some take a religious approach, believing that the one-world government conspiracy is maintained by and for a group of people who serve Satan and is to bring about the end of the world. They feel that one of the goals of the one-world government is to merge all religions into a one-world church, the goal of which will be to serve Satan. Some feel that the New Age movements are a part of this.

Another main goal of the conspiracy is said to be control of all the world's money. Believers feel that if the elite group controls the money, they control the people and that this is done with debt. The elite are keeping everyone else in debt to them, which keeps the people under their control. They believe that the elite is controlling our money because if we have the financial resources, we have the power to fight back, but if they keep us destitute and under their thumb financially, we'll be too dependent on them to try to overthrow them. They also feel that the elite are keeping us poor, so we have to keep working harder and harder, longer and longer hours. The busier and more exhausted we are because of the work we need to do just to get by, the less likely we are to revolt.

Believers also say that this group of elites creates problems on purpose to keep us distracted and worn out, like wars and market depressions. They say this is to confuse and distract us, so we won't be paying attention to their actions. According to believers, this group funded both sides of most of the wars that have been fought during the last 200 years. The weather is also under this group's control and is manipulated for their gain.   The group is said to control disease and medicine, to give the powerful more control over the weaker masses.

Signs that believers say point to the world being pushed into a one-world government include the movement toward globalization, foreign investment, free trade, international organizations, peace agreements that give a false sense of security, privatization, and debt.

Conclusion

Thank for making it through to the end of this book, let's hope it was informative.

I hope you walk away from reading this book with some knowledge that you didn't have before, and a thirst to learn more. You may not believe anything about the theories that you have learned about, but something might have had a ring of truth to it, and if that is the case, I encourage you to do more research and see for yourself. Who knows? The truth may be out there.

Finally, if you found this book useful in any way, a review on Amazon is always appreciated!

25704287R00050